CREATIVE FUND-RAISING

Mary Ann Burke
Carl Liljenstolpe

A FIFTY-MINUTE™ SERIES BOOK

CRISP PUBLICATIONS, INC.
Menlo Park, California

CREATIVE FUND-RAISING

Mary Ann Burke
and Carl Liljenstolpe

CREDITS:
Editor: **Brenda Machosky**
Designer: **Carol Harris**
Typesetting: **ExecuStaff**
Cover Design: **Carol Harris**
Artwork: **Ralph Mapson**

Copyright © 1993 Crisp Publications, Inc.
Printed in the United States of America by Bawden Printing Company.

English language Crisp books are distributed worldwide. Our major international distributors include:

CANADA: Reid Publishing, Ltd., Box 69559—109 Thomas St., Oakville, Ontario Canada L6J 7R4. TEL: (416) 842-4428; FAX: (416) 842-9327

AUSTRALIA: Career Builders, P.O. Box 1051, Springwood, Brisbane, Queensland, Australia 4127. TEL: 841-1061, FAX: 841-1580

NEW ZEALAND: Career Builders, P.O. Box 571, Manurewa, Auckland, New Zealand. TEL: 266-5276, FAX: 266-4152

JAPAN: Phoenix Associates Co., Mizuho Bldg. 2-12-2, Kami Osaki, Shinagawa-Ku, Tokyo 141, Japan. TEL: 3-443-7231, FAX: 3-443-7640

Selected Crisp titles are also available in other languages. Contact International Rights Manager Tim Polk at (800) 442-7477 for more information.

Library of Congress Catalog Card Number 92-054369
Burke, Mary Ann and Carl Liljenstolpe
Creative Fund-Raising
ISBN 1-56052-181-3

This book is printed on recyclable paper with soy ink.

PREFACE

As traditional funding sources become scarce, creative fund-raising is critical for an organization's survival. Organizations are developing comprehensive long range fund-raising plans in order to guarantee their economic well-being.

Effective fund-raising plans require diversified strategies for expanding and nurturing the organization's donors. This book will provide you with strategies, examples and worksheets on how to:

> Identify Fund-Raising Sources
> Nurture and Develop Donors
> Produce Special Events
> Create a Donor Development Center
> Solicit Donations
> Create a Long Range Fund-Raising Plan
> Utilize Resources Creatively

If you plan to expand your fund-raising activities, this book will guide you in developing effective strategies.

This book can also assist you in:

> Assessing Your Fund-Raising Activities
> Considering Innovative Fund-Raising Strategies
> Expanding the Development of Your Donors
> Planning and Effectively Utilizing Resources

Regardless of your past fund-raising experiences, this book will help you identify an appropriate variety of strategies. These strategies can be uniquely designed to meet the diverse needs of your organization and your donor population.

Carl A. Liljenstolpe   Mary Ann Burke

ABOUT THIS BOOK

Creative Fund-Raising is not like most books. It has a unique "self-study" format that encourages a reader to become personally involved. Designed to be "read with a pencil," there is an abundance of exercises, activities, assessments and cases that invite participation.

The objective of this book is to help organizations and companies to assess their fund-raising needs, identify and nurture donors and implement various strategies and activities that will raise the needed funds.

Creative Fund-Raising (and the other self-improvement books listed in the back of this book) can be used effectively in a number of ways. Here are some possibilities:

—**Individual Study.** Because the book is self-instructional, all that is needed is a quiet place, some time and a pencil. By completing the activities and exercises, a reader should not only receive valuable feedback, but also practical steps in creative fund-raising.

—**Workshops and Seminars.** The book is ideal for reading prior to a workshop or seminar. With the basics in hand, the quality of participation will improve. More time can be spent on concept extensions and applications during the program. The book is also effective when a trainer distributes it at the beginning of a session and leads participants through the contents.

—**Remote Location Training.** Copies can be sent to those not able to attend "home office" training sessions.

—**Informal Study Groups.** Thanks to the format, brevity and low cost, this book is ideal for "brown-bag" or other informal group sessions.

There are other possibilities that depend on the objectives, program or ideas of the user. One thing for sure, even after it has been read, this book will serve as excellent reference material that can be easily reviewed.

ACKNOWLEDGMENTS

We would like to thank Barbara Titel for creating the following graphics:

> The donor development center information chart
>
> The buying motives of personality types diagram
>
> The checklist to identify telephone personalities

Additional thanks goes to Carl Mehl from the Planned Giving Foundation in San Jose, California for contributing to the charitable trust case study and worksheet.

Finally, thanks to the publishers, Mike Crisp and Phil Gerould, for their attentive guidance and support throughout the project.

ABOUT THE AUTHORS

Mary Ann Burke is the principal owner of Novation Associates, a nonprofit consulting firm located in Los Gatos, California. During the last decade, Mary Ann has provided technical assistance in fund-raising, volunteer development, strategic planning and community problem solving to various organizations. In addition, she has offered adult education classes in volunteer development, public relations, human development, self-esteem, and career assessment. Mary Ann studied Public Administration and holds an M.A. in Educational Administration.

Carl Liljenstolpe has owned and operated his own companies for over twenty years. Initially, Carl worked in the office equipment industry. In 1990, Carl founded Profit Technology in Los Gatos, California and cofounded Tactix Marketing Technologies in Omaha, Nebraska. Both firms specialize in implementing customer development and sales automation systems for commercial corporate accounts. In addition to consulting, Carl has held various nonprofit leadership roles. He has a B.A. in Marketing.

In their work, Carl and Mary Ann have discovered that a wealth of fund-raising and donor development opportunities are available through appropriate strategic planning and marketing.

Carl and Mary Ann are the authors of *Recruiting Volunteers: A Guide for Nonprofits,* also published by Crisp Publications. The authors welcome your comments and questions. You can reach them at:

Profit Technology
200 Mistletoe Road
Los Gatos, CA 95030
Phone: (408) 866-4990
Fax: (408) 866-4718

CONTENTS

CONTENTS (continued)

INTRODUCTION

As summarized below, *Creative Fund-Raising* will take you through the methodical process of defining fund-raising within an organization, identifying grant sources, developing donors through special events and the Donor Development Center, and evaluating other types of donations.

Finally, you will design your own practical fund-raising plan for the solicitation and creative utilization of resources.

SECTION 1—What Is Fund-Raising?

Using a variety of work sheets, you will evaluate your current fund-raising strategies. This information will enable you to assess how to further diversify your fund-raising plan.

SECTION 2—Grant Development

Completing the work sheets will give you the opportunity to identify appropriate grant sources for your organization's programs.

SECTION 3—Donor Development Methods

Once you assess various donor development and special events strategies, you will be able to determine the appropriate methods and events for nurturing your donors.

SECTION 4—Creation of a Donor Development Center (DDC)

You can systematically nurture and develop your donors by creating and maintaining in a donor computer database.

SECTION 5—Planned Giving and Charitable Trusts

Learn how planned giving can provide substantial long-term donor contributions to your organization.

SECTION 6—Soliciting for Other Types of Donations

By considering different types of donations, you can strategically solicit for a variety of donated products and services.

INTRODUCTION (continued)

SECTION 7—Creating a Long Range Fund-Raising Plan

The work sheets will help you determine your immediate fund-raising strategies and your fund-raising plans for the future.

SECTION 8—The Creative Utilization of Resources

Donors and community resources are limited. You will learn how to utilize scarce resources more creatively to meet the diverse needs of your organization and your donors.

SECTION

1

What Is Fund-Raising?

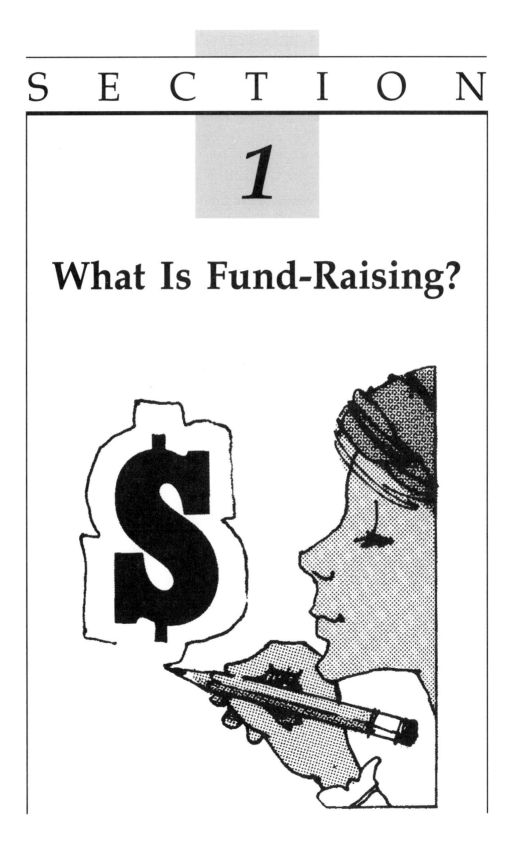

WHAT IS FUND-RAISING?

The first section in this book is designed to help you understand your perception of your current fund-raising strategies. With this information, you will be able to assess how you can further develop your fund-raising program.

Organizations with diversified fund-raising and donor development strategies can benefit in the following ways:

- As the organization applies to new sources for diversified funding, its mission and services are publicized.

- An organization can recruit new volunteers for fund-raising and support services as it makes appeals for funding.

- An organization can generate other resources or gifts-in-kind from prospective funders or donors.

- When soliciting funds, an organization can educate community members.

- Informed donors will know about the benefits of various human services for themselves and for others.

- Knowledgeable funders and donors are more likely to contribute extensive resources in response to a specific community need.

- Nurtured funders and donors are more likely to fund new services within the organization.

- Funders and donors are more responsive to an organization that solicits funding from a variety of sources.

- Special events can nurture donors, educate the community, fund-raise and recruit volunteers.

- Fund-raising events offer ample opportunities for organizations to solicit other types of donations and build relationships with the community merchants.

- An enlightened community and educated donors are empowered to respond to human needs!

- Fund-raising is not just soliciting money, but also gaining recognition, community support, and nonmonetary donations.

Fund-raising is not just soliciting money, but also gaining recognition, community support, and nonmonetary donations. Fund-raising and soliciting money from various sources is becoming more challenging, creative and labor intensive. Organizations must strategically plan to diversify their funding sources and to fully develop their relationships with individual donors.

EVALUATING YOUR FUND-RAISING STRATEGIES

List your organization's current fund-raising strategies or activities.

_____

_____

_____

_____

_____

List your organization's various funding sources.

_____

_____

_____

_____

_____

List your organization's strategies for fully developing your relationships with donors.

_____

_____

_____

_____

_____

List your organization's special events.

_____

_____

_____

_____

_____

List the other types of donations your organization receives.

_____

_____

_____

_____

_____

List specific strategies or activities for fund-raising you want to develop or expand in your organization.

_____

_____

_____

_____

_____

EVALUATING YOUR FUND-RAISING STRATEGIES (continued)

Consider the previous benefits identified through diversified fund-raising and donor development strategies. List the three primary fund-raising benefits which your organization should focus on developing.

1. _____

_____

2. _____

_____

3. _____

_____

List any other benefits you would like to include in your fund-raising strategies:

_____

_____

_____

_____

_____

You will be able to consider innovative fund-raising and donor development strategies in the next few pages. This information will help your organization respond to the diverse needs of your funders and donor population.

SECTION

2

Grant Development

GRANT DEVELOPMENT

Funding sources are overwhelmed with grant requests as traditional funding sources diminish. The funding organizations are responding to this crisis by:

1. Requiring more financial and performance documentation from an organization seeking funding

2. Prioritizing critical community needs

3. Determining criteria to meet community needs

4. Refusing to fund certain needs

The next few pages will help you identify appropriate grant funding sources for your organization's programs. Additional funding sources in the community can be identified through funding publications. Contact your local community library, college library or nonprofit reference library for a list of funding publications.

After you determine which organizations might fund your program, phone each funder to discuss how your program might fit the organization's funding criteria. If the funder is interested in your proposal, you will be asked to complete a grant application packet or submit a letter of inquiry.

GOVERNMENT ORGANIZATIONS

Local, state and federal government organizations can provide ample funding for specific projects, contracts or a community need. Available government funding sources can be identified by:

► Contacting governmental organizations that provide support in your field of service.

► Contacting organizations in your field of service that are receiving government funding and asking them for government organization referrals or project collaboration.

► Contacting local universities, libraries and nonprofit development organizations for referrals and publications that advertise government funding.

► Subscribing to publications that announce various government grants.

Once you have identified appropriate government funding sources, request the funding applications and guidelines. Completely review the funding guidelines and criteria used to determine funding decisions. Many governmental organization grant guidelines encourage community collaboration for coordination of resources. Consider modifying your program plan to meet the funding criteria and community collaboration. Government organizations, nonprofit development organizations, and fund-raising consultants are available to provide technical assistance and training for completing government grant applications.

GOVERNMENT FUNDING ASSESSMENT

GOVERNMENT ORGANIZATIONS FUNDING ASSESSMENT

1. Consider at least one service that your organization currently provides or would like to develop that could qualify for government funding.

   _____

   _____

   _____

2. How do you plan to identify governmental sources of funding for this service?

   _____

   _____

   _____

3. How can you modify the service to collaborate and share resources with other organizations?

   _____

   _____

   _____

4. List the organizations you plan to contact for this collaboration and the resources each organization can provide.

   _____

   _____

   _____

5. Do you need technical assistance to complete the grant application and who will you contact for this assistance?

   _____

   _____

   _____

PRIVATE FOUNDATIONS

Private foundations are nonprofit organizations that provide funding to tax-exempt organizations for human services, research, education, the arts and community projects. Foundations that fund specific projects can be identified by:

► Contacting organizations and organizations in your field of service for referrals.

► Contacting local libraries, colleges, and nonprofit development organizations for referrals or publications.

► Subscribing to fund development and grant writing periodicals.

► Contacting your local community foundation or other foundations in your community for referrals.

After you collect a list of prospective foundations, contact each foundation and ask for an annual report and the current proposal guidelines. Review the annual report and grant guidelines to determine if the foundation funds the type of program you plan to propose. Smaller foundations may not have specific grant guidelines and may ask you to submit a brief summary about the project.

Most foundations will require the following information about an organization and a proposed program. Check off each item as it is prepared.

☐ The organization's mission statement.

☐ The organization's address, phone number, and a contact name.

☐ A proposed program description.

☐ The program's goals and objectives. The goals should define the proposed program's results and the objectives should describe the means of obtaining the proposed results.

☐ A proposed evaluation plan for determining if the objectives have been achieved.

☐ A budget that lists the program expenses and revenues.

☐ A description about collaborative efforts, matching funds and gifts-in-kind.

☐ Community demographics and client statistics.

☐ A Board of Directors roster.

☐ Copies of the organization's federal and state tax exempt status.

☐ A copy of the organization's articles of incorporation and bylaws.

PRIVATE FOUNDATION FUNDING ASSESSMENT

1. Describe the program you plan to expand or develop to meet an emerging community need.

_____

_____

_____

_____

2. How do you plan to identify appropriate private foundation funding for the proposed program?

_____

_____

_____

3. After reviewing various private foundation guidelines, to which foundations are you going to submit proposals?

_____

_____

_____

_____

4. List the organizations, companies and individuals you plan to contact for collaboration, gifts-in-kind and matching funds.

_____

_____

_____

_____

CORPORATIONS

Companies can offer tremendous financial support and resources to the community. Company contributions can include:

► Funding for human services and community projects.

► Sponsoring nonprofit fund-raising and community service events.

► Loaning employees to assist in nonprofit fund-raising and community service events.

► Providing technical assistance and equipment for a nonprofit activity.

► Donating facilities for the organization's use.

► Providing food and training to community organizations.

► Donating company products and services to fund-raising events.

► Donating used equipment and company products to organizations.

► Promoting nonprofit organizations or human services in a company fund-raising campaign.

► Educating employees about organizations and their programs in company publications and presentations.

An organization must be flexible, creative and resourceful when approaching a company for funding, donations, or services. Ideally, the organization should present a proposal to a company that not only will benefit the organization, but also will benefit the company. Once an organization has developed a healthy relationship with a company, the organization and the company will have ample opportunities for future collaborations.

CORPORATE FUNDING EXAMPLES AND ASSESSMENT

Consider the following beneficial company and nonprofit funding collaborations:

COLLABORATION #1:

Challenge High School District had recently purchased a computer system for their schools and their district office from Able Computer Company. After considering the vocational needs of its students, the District decided to develop a vocational training center. Able Computer Company funded the project and provided the computers for the center. In addition, the company featured the project as their commitment to the community in several periodical advertisements. This donation benefited the company, the school district, and the students.

COLLABORATION #2:

Talking Tales Agency is a nonprofit organization that provides public speaking training to community members. Each week the organization holds its meeting at Cecil's Coffee House. The restaurant provides free use of its facility and a 10% discount for food purchased by the organization's participants. Talking Tales Agency promotes the restaurant's contributions in their community recruiting literature.

COLLABORATION #3:

Gusto Computers significantly contributes to its community. After reviewing several nonprofit proposals, the company chose to support the Volunteer Agency's Donor Center by donating computer equipment, technical assistance, and staff funding. The Donor Center advertised Gusto Computer's contribution and Gusto Computer featured the Volunteer Agency's Donor Center in its advertisements.

YOUR COLLABORATION EXAMPLE:

Consider the previous examples and identify one company in your community that you can approach for a beneficial contribution. Describe the donation and benefits for each partner in the space provided.

_____

_____

_____

OTHER SOURCES

Other funding sources include professional organizations, service groups, educational institutions, church groups, labor unions and merchant associations. These groups can provide financial support, research assistance, facilities, labor, product donations and promotional support.

Consider and describe a service your organization currently offers or plans to develop.

_____

_____

How can the following groups help you to provide program services?

Professional Organizations

_____

_____

Service Groups

_____

_____

Educational Institutions

_____

_____

Church Groups

_____

_____

Labor Unions

_____

_____

Merchant Associations

_____

_____

MATCHING FUNDS

Many government, private foundations, and corporate funders require equivalent funding from another source as a condition for funding.

For example, a corporate funder will agree to give $10,000 to an organization if the organization can assure the company that it can obtain an additional $10,000 from another funding source. In another situation, a private funder may require that the organization assures the private funder that it will equally fund a proposed project.

Sources for matching funds can be identified through publications at local libraries, college libraries, and through regional fund-raising reference libraries.

List the various funding sources available for a program in your organization.

1. _____

2. _____

3. _____

4. _____

5. _____

6. _____

7. _____

8. _____

9. _____

10. _____

Describe how you can receive matching funds for your project from different sources.

_____

_____

_____

_____

S E C T I O N

3

Traditional Donor Development Tactics

TRADITIONAL DONOR DEVELOPMENT TACTICS

Developing and nurturing your relationships with donors is critical for an organization's survival. Informed and knowledgeable donors can:

- ✔ Promote and advertise your organization's programs to friends and the community

- ✔ Educate the community about the human service needs your organization supports

- ✔ Provide testimony about your organization's successful experiences

- ✔ Network with other community members for recruiting volunteers

- ✔ Solicit donations for organization programs and special events

- ✔ Increase their level of giving

- ✔ Encourage colleagues to increase their levels of giving

- ✔ Match contributions with other donors

- ✔ Become organization volunteers

- ✔ Become recipients of organization services

In this section you will explore various strategies for recruiting donors and for nurturing ongoing relationships with them.

DIRECT MAIL

The direct mail solicitation* is a fund-raising method for contacting a large number of donors or prospective donors with a specific message. A direct mail solicitation is a method for:

► Educating the donor or prospective donor about the organization and its services

► Collecting donor or prospective donor information

► Fund-raising

Mailers used by organizations include personal letters, reply cards, organization service brochures, organization literature, catalogues and information books. Direct mail solicitations can be followed through with a personal phone call. The phone call is an ideal way to send another piece of correspondence. Direct mail solicitations without names are a waste of postage.

Benefits include:

1. A *specific message is received* by a large number of donors or prospective donors.

2. The organization has *high visibility*.

3. *Profits* are achieved.

4. Clients that respond can be developed for a *higher level of support and giving*.

Limitations include:

1. There is a *low return* for the investment.

2. A *high level of sophistication* is required to be successful.

3. The process is *labor intensive*.

4. *Less than 1%* of the new prospective donors will respond with a donation.

For large direct mail campaigns and for direct mail strategies, please refer to *Direct Mail Magic,* Crisp Publications. This publication can help you understand the complexity of various direct mail strategies, how to develop an effective direct mail campaign, and how to measure results.

DIRECT MAIL WORKSHEET

List the different direct mail strategies that your organization initiated in the last year.

_____

_____

_____

_____

_____

_____

How successful were these ventures?

_____

_____

_____

_____

_____

_____

Should your organization consider additional direct mail campaigns?

_____

_____

_____

_____

_____

COMPANY CAMPAIGNS

Company campaigns have greatly increased as more companies commit resources to their communities. Companies vary in their commitment of resources to fund-raising activities. The following examples illustrate this diversity:

| *Example 1:* | **Personal Check from Company President** |

Each fall Richardson's Accounting Firm asks six organizations in its community to make a human service presentation at the company. After the presentation, the company president donates $1,000 to each participating organization.

| *Example 2:* | **Matching Gift** |

Rush Advertising runs a display ad in a local newspaper for ten human service organizations in the community. The company commits to matching all the money that has been raised from the ad. The ad raises $10,000 in contributions and the company matches this with another $10,000 donation.

| *Example 3:* | **Corporate Gift** |

Thomas Engineering offers a health and safety wellness conference to its employees each year. Local organizations provide the presenters for the conference. The company contributes $2,000 to each organization that makes a presentation.

| *Example 4:* | **Mail Campaign** |

Doyle Design Associates coordinates a mail campaign for its employees and distributes a human service solicitation memo with each employee's payroll check. Employees have an opportunity to make a one-time contribution or have a monthly amount of money deducted from their payroll check for a specific organization.

| *Example 5:* | **Staff Meeting Campaign** |

The City of El Gato sponsors an extensive fund-raising campaign among its employees. The mayor and a human service organization make a presentation at the weekly staff meeting. After the presentation, pledge cards to support community human services are distributed to all employees. A follow-up memo for the campaign is distributed later in the week. Employee coordinators contact employees that have not responded to the memo. The city tracks its campaign results with a goal-setting chart. The final day of the campaign is celebrated with an employee picnic.

COMPANY CAMPAIGN SAMPLE PLAN

Consider the various company campaign examples described on the previous page. In the spaces provided, answer the following questions and create a sample company campaign plan for your organization.

Which companies in your community would your organization approach for a company campaign?

_____

_____

_____

Would your organization consider collaborating with other organizations or nonprofit fund-raisers for this campaign?

_____

If you answered yes on the previous question, how would your organization collaborate with other organizations on this fund-raising strategy?

_____

_____

_____

_____

Describe the type of company campaign that you feel would best meet the needs of your organization and the prospective companies that you have identified.

_____

_____

_____

_____

CAPITAL CAMPAIGNS

Organizations need fund-raising strategies for capital expenditures as well as for their day-to-day operations. Consider the following capital campaign projects that local communities have planned:

► A nonprofit organization that provides family education classes and vocational counseling to unemployed women is raising funds through corporate sponsorships for single parent housing. The housing units will be built above their existing facility. The organization will provide child care and parent support services to the housing residents.

► A mental health organization for severely emotionally disturbed adults is soliciting corporate matching funds for a cluster housing project. The project will provide long-term, independent housing with facilities for ongoing emotional and vocational counseling.

► A church is recruiting donor-sponsors for organizing a community school where various social service organizations can provide direct services to neighborhood families. The neighborhood facility would provide child care, health and dental care services, emotional and vocational counseling, family support services, vocational training and recreational classes to local residents.

► A community health clinic is raising funds through planned-giving to expand its facility for providing dental care services, AIDS education and family life support services.

In the spaces provided consider what capital campaign project your organization may want to develop.

_____

_____

Identify four fund-raising strategies for developing your capital campaign.

1. _____

2. _____

3. _____

4. _____

PRODUCING SPECIAL EVENTS

Special events offer your organization ample opportunities to:

► Promote and advertise your organization's services to the community.

► Educate the community about the human service needs your organization supports.

► Recruit new organization volunteers.

► Recruit additional resources for your services.

► Recruit new donors and increase your donors' current level of giving.

In the next few pages you will have an opportunity to explore various strategies for creating and implementing the following special events:

- Silent Auctions
- Dinners and Entertainment
- Sports Tournaments
- Sales of Products
- Raffles

- Carnivals
- Home Tours
- Telethons
- Sport-A-Thons
- Discount Booklets

When reviewing these various events for your organization, realistically consider your organization's staff, volunteers and community contacts for resources.

SILENT AUCTIONS

Silent auctions have become increasingly popular in recent years. A silent auction will provide the participant with a description book of all the items that the participant can bid on. A fee is charged to obtain the silent auction book.

At a typical silent auction, the items that will be auctioned can be viewed by the participants throughout the event. Participants can submit a bid on an item during the event until a specific table of items is closed to bidding. At the time of closing the person with the highest bid will buy the item.

The following are typical silent auction donations:

- Vacation rentals and trips
- Restaurant gift certificates
- Gift certificates for services and products
- Gift certificates that can be redeemed for professional services
- Autographed sports equipment and clothing
- Computer equipment, office machines
- Toys
- Art
- Collector's books
- Airplane rides
- Jewelry
- Kitchen appliances
- Entertainment gift certificates
- Building materials
- Dining with celebrities

Silent auctions can also include a combination of the following fund-raising strategies:

✓ A pre-auction barbecue or meal ticket that can be purchased separately. The meal ticket can include raffle prizes that will be presented at the auction.

✓ A wine tasting of regional wines. This event can take place before or during the silent auction.

✓ A sampling of regional cuisine offered by local restaurants. The food can be purchased before and during the auction.

✓ A sampling of desserts prepared by local bakeries.

✓ A cook-off event or food festival before the auction. Popular cook-off events have included regional favorites such as chili, garlic, artichokes, and pumpkin.

✓ A progressive dinner preceding the event at local restaurants or homes.

✓ Sales of organization cookbooks, calendars and greeting cards, clients' arts and crafts, a publication of clients' writing selections.

✓ Sales of raffle tickets for items that will be awarded during the auction.

✓ Sales of treasure chest keys that can open a grand prize treasure chest at the event.

✓ Sales of tickets to upcoming organization events.

SILENT AUCTION WORKSHEET

Design your own unique silent auction event in the spaces provided.

What resources do you have to organize a silent auction?

_____

_____

_____

What type of event would you plan before the silent auction?

_____

_____

What donations can you solicit from the community for this event?

_____

_____

_____

Who do you know that can help you with the auction publications, advertising materials and tickets?

_____

_____

What public relations contacts have you developed for this event?

_____

_____

Do you know anyone who can provide financial services and accounting support for the event?

_____

_____

How much money do you plan to raise at the event?

_____

DINNERS AND ENTERTAINMENT

Fund-raising dinners and entertainment are relatively common special events for most nonprofits. Dinners can be as simple as receiving partial credit for pizzas purchased from a pizza parlor or as sophisticated as paying $100 per plate at a formal dinner with dancing. A tremendous amount of money can be raised depending on the type of event. Review the following descriptions of other types of fund-raising dinners and entertainment:

- Restaurant gift certificates that donate the cost of a second dinner to a nonprofit

- Entertainment gift certificates that donate the cost of a second admission fee to a nonprofit

- Annual business dinners

- Volunteer recognition events that are sponsored by local companies

- Progressive dinners at local restaurants or homes

- Pot luck dinners

- International dinners provided by local ethnic restaurants with entertainment provided by local ethnic musicians

- Community music festivals

- Community air shows

- Boat dances

- Volunteer and staff reunion dinners

- Membership recruitment dinners

- Sporting events

- Performing arts education and open houses at the library and museums

- Fashion shows and luncheons

DINNERS AND ENTERTAINMENT WORKSHEET

Organize your next dinner and entertainment fund-raising event in the spaces provided.

Who will organize the event?

_____

_____

What resources can be donated for the event?

_____

_____

_____

When and where will the event take place?

_____

_____

Will you combine various types of eating experiences or entertainment at the event?

_____

_____

Are there other goals you wish to accomplish at this event besides fund-raising?

_____

_____

How will you include these goals at your event?

_____

_____

What advertising and public relations contacts will you use for the event?

_____

_____

SPORTS TOURNAMENTS

Sports tournaments are a major fund-raiser for some nonprofits. Fund-raising sports tournaments include golf, tennis and bowling. Tournament participants pay a fee to play and the top winners win monetary awards. Free promotional sports items are usually distributed at the event.

Many sports tournaments incorporate some or all of the following fund-raising activities:

- Music

- Raffles

- Sports demonstrations

- Food sales, catered meals

- Sales of promotional sports items

- Sales of the organization's calendars

- Celebrities autographing sports paraphernalia

- Sales of tickets to upcoming organization events

- Sales of items made by the organization for the event

- Sales of human service community resource publications

SPORTS TOURNAMENTS WORKSHEET

Consider the type of sports tournament your organization can sponsor in the spaces provided.

What sports facilities are accessible for your use?

_____

_____

Do you have any sports contacts that can help you organize a tournament?

_____

_____

_____

What additional fund-raising activities would you include at the tournament?

_____

_____

What donations can you solicit from the community for the additional activities?

_____

_____

Who can help you with the printing, advertising and publicity?

_____

_____

What companies in your community would help you sponsor the event?

_____

_____

Which sports celebrities can help you promote the event?

_____

SALES OF PRODUCTS

Nonprofits have ample opportunities to sell a variety of products at cost or to create their own products. Organizations sell products for the following reasons:

► To raise funds

► To advertise their services

► To educate the community about the needs of their clients

► To educate the community about when a person can benefit from a service

► To raise awareness about a social problem

► To recruit volunteers

► To solicit other community donations

Products sold by organizations can be made by the staff, can be created by the clients and volunteers or can be purchased wholesale for resale. Review the following product list and consider the diversity of products that a nonprofit can sell.

- Publications
- Stationery supplies
- Arts and crafts
- Calendars
- Clothing advertising the organization
- Organization mugs, glasses, vases

- Organization windshield sun screens
- Organization key chains
- Organization desk accessories
- Jewelry
- Candy, nuts, delicatessen specialties
- Sports and health accessories

SALES OF PRODUCTS WORKSHEET

List which products your organization can create to sell.

_____

_____

List which products your organization would consider selling for fund-raising and advertising?

_____

_____

Does your organization have any distributor or product contacts?

_____

_____

List organizations that have successfully sold products for fund-raising.

_____

_____

Who are the product sources for these organizations?

_____

_____

Do you have any duplicating, advertising and public relations contacts?

_____

_____

How can you educate the community about your services and needs through this fund-raising strategy?

_____

_____

How much money do you plan to raise from these activities?

_____

RAFFLES

Raffles require minimal time for fund-raising and can furnish substantial profits. Most raffles offer a variety of donated or partially donated prizes. Tickets can be purchased individually or several can be purchased at a discount. Popular raffle prizes can include the following:

- Cars
- Vacations or trips
- Money
- Gift certificates
- Vacation days from work
- Television sets
- Computers
- Walkman radios
- Sports equipment
- Sports events passes

- Outdoor adventures
- Entertainment passes
- Consulting services
- Books
- Arts and crafts
- Toys
- Stereos
- Appliances
- Furniture
- Clothing
- Jewelry

We Won! We Won!

RAFFLE WORKSHEET

List the donations you can solicit for a raffle.

_____

_____

_____

_____

When will the raffle take place?

_____

What other fund-raising activities will you include at the raffle?

_____

_____

_____

Who can provide donations for these additional activities?

_____

_____

Who will sell the raffle tickets and how will you distribute them to these people?

_____

_____

Will you provide sales incentive prizes and what will these be?

_____

Who can donate printing and duplicating services?

_____

_____

What advertising and public relations contacts have you developed for this event?

_____

CARNIVALS

Carnivals have the potential of raising large sums of money when various fund-raising strategies are included in the project. Most nonprofits rent the carnival rides and some of the games from a commercial carnival supplier.

A few carnival suppliers provide all the games, rides, and most of the food. In this situation, the nonprofit must sell large quantities of advance ride tickets to reap a significant fund-raising profit.

Consider the following additional types of fund-raising activities you can include at your carnival:

- Raffle opportunities when purchasing a full book of ride tickets

- Prizes for the persons selling the most advance tickets

- Sales of organization publications, arts and crafts

- Celebrities autographing memorabilia

- Barbecue lunches and dinners

- Sports demonstrations

- Human resource fair

- Pie eating contests

- Haunted houses

- Musical concerts

- Face decorating

- Puppet shows

- Relay contests

- Wellness fair

- Magic shows

- Comedians

- Balloon art

- Clowns

CARNIVAL WORKSHEET

Who do you plan to contract with for the carnival rides?

_____

What other services does the carnival supplier offer?

_____

_____

_____

What six additional activities do you plan to include at the carnival?

_____   _____

_____   _____

_____   _____

What donations can you solicit from the community for these activities?

_____

_____

_____

Who can help you with printing the tickets and the promotional materials?

_____

Who can help you with the advertising and public relations?

_____

Which community groups can help you with the event?

_____

_____

_____

How much money do you plan to raise from the event?

_____

HOME TOURS

Home tour fund-raising events offer the community several unique benefits. Home tours can:

► Showcase historical buildings and homes in the community

► Feature various architectural designs

► Display homes that were extensively remodeled or refurbished

► Feature homes with unique floor plans

► Showcase homes with energy saving features

► Advertise homes with unique interior decorating themes

► Display homes with various space-saving additions

► Show homes with attractive ornamental gardens and landscaping

Home tour fund-raising projects can also include the following types of fund-raising activities:

• Progressive dinners can be provided with each course served at a different home.

• An educational preview can be offered at a home tour site.

• A barbecue or dinner can be served at the organization or at a historical restaurant before the tour.

• Home furnishings can be raffled as prizes.

• Each tour site can sell home tour memorabilia.

• A musical concert can be presented at a home tour site.

• An art and wine festival can be offered at a home tour site.

• A silent auction for home furnishings can be featured at a home tour site.

• Tickets to future nonprofit events can be sold.

HOME TOUR WORKSHEET

What is your home tour theme?

_____

List ten homes that you would like to feature for a home tour fund-raising event.

1. _____   2. _____

3. _____   4. _____

5. _____   6. _____

7. _____   8. _____

9. _____   10. _____

Who can design brochures for the home tour?

_____

What other fund-raising activities will you include with the home tour?

_____

_____

What donations can you solicit for the event?

_____

_____

Who can help you with printing and duplicating?

_____

What advertising and public relations contacts do you have?

_____

_____

Which service groups can help you with the event?

_____

_____

TELETHONS

Telethons educate the community about a human service need through media coverage, celebrity entertainment, testimonials and fund-raising activities. Telethons tend to be most successful when organized by a major nonprofit or when sponsored by several nonprofits in a community.

Most telethons are televised programs. The goal is to motivate television viewers to phone the program and commit a financial pledge. Other telethons motivate television viewers to commit volunteer hours, services or product donations for a particular human service cause.

Regardless of the plea for help, telethons are big business and require a tremendous amount of community support and resources. Identify the type of telethon your organization can organize in the spaces provided.

What organizations would your organization collaborate with for a telethon and how much money would you want to raise?

_____

_____

Who do you know in the community that can help you develop a telethon?

_____

_____

Do you know any celebrities, television personalities or media organizers that can help you organize the event?

_____

_____

Who would help you publicize the event?

_____

What service groups can help you staff the phones?

_____

Who can provide you with bookkeeping and accounting assistance?

_____

SPORT-A-THONS

Sport-a-thon activities have grown in popularity and diversity. Activities include:

- ✓ Swimming
- ✓ Basketball
- ✓ Batting
- ✓ Bowling
- ✓ Jumping rope
- ✓ Jogging or walking
- ✓ Bicycling

- ✓ Track activities
- ✓ Dancing
- ✓ Skate boarding
- ✓ Sit-ups
- ✓ Chin-ups
- ✓ Pull-ups
- ✓ Tennis

Before participating in an event, sport-a-thon participants solicit pledges from sponsors for the number of laps they may swim or for the number of hours they can dance without stopping. If a sponsor pledges fifty cents for each swimming lap, the athlete will receive thirty dollars for completing sixty laps.

List three types of activities your organization can coordinate for soliciting pledges from sponsors.

1. _____

_____

_____

2. _____

_____

_____

3. _____

_____

_____

DISCOUNT BOOKLETS

Discount booklets are an easy fund-raising activity for nonprofit organizations. Discount booklets can include coupons for:

- Meals
- Hotels and lodging
- Rental cars
- Entertainment

- Services
- Packaged trips
- Products
- Sporting events

There are companies that sell packaged discount booklets to nonprofits for fund-raising. The nonprofit can resell the booklets for a profit. Organizations can also create their own discount booklets by soliciting discounts from local merchants. Certificates are created to advertise the merchant's discount and are bound into a book to be sold for a profit.

Identify two companies that offer packaged discount booklets:

1. _____

2. _____

List ten local merchants that can provide discount certificates to your organization:

1. _____   2. _____

3. _____   4. _____

5. _____   6. _____

7. _____   8. _____

9. _____   10. _____

SECTION

4

Creation of a Donor Development Center

CREATION OF A DONOR DEVELOPMENT CENTER

Your organization can develop a Donor Development Center (DDC) by creating a computerized marketing database for donors and corporate donors. Through the use of database relationship marketing software, you can:

☐ Create an easy and low-cost central database of donors' and corporate donors' information.

☐ Document donors' and corporate donors' perceived interests and needs.

☐ Create message-specific correspondence with individual donors or corporate donors at systematic predetermined times.

Your organization has an 80 percent chance of increasing a donor's or corporate donor's commitment to fund-raising, volunteering or donating resources because you can customize correspondence according to perceived interests and needs. The DDC can also support the following fund-raising activities:

- The DDC can manage donors and prospects through the contact and qualifying stages of the soliciting process.

- The DDC can build relationships between your organization, and its donors and corporate donors.

- The DDC can collect and use the database in a cost effective and timely way to create opportunities for increased contributions.

- The DDC can transfer the donor or corporate donor to a fund-raising volunteer at an appropriate point in the solicitation process.

- The DDC accurately and consistently keeps track of each donor and corporate donor.

STEPS FOR CREATING THE DDC

There are five essential steps for creating the DDC:

STEP 1: Develop the DDC Team

The DDC requires staff, computer technology, a telephone and a quiet work area.

STEP 2: Establish the DDC Database

Define the type of information you will collect for the database and determine if you will set up different databases for specific groups or needs.

STEP 3: Identify the DDC Target Groups

Consider the various donor groups and identify the donors and prospective donors.

STEP 4: Determine What Information Is Valuable

Determine what information you will collect for donors and corporate donors.

STEP 5: Strategies for Collecting Information

Survey data can be compiled for the DDC through various strategies.

THE FIVE-STEP PROGRAM

STEP 1: DEVELOP THE DDC TEAM

The Donor Development Center requires the following support and equipment:

1. The DDC representative or volunteers should be goal oriented, inquisitive, poised, socially adept, intelligent, self-confident, enthusiastic, honest, computer literate, have the ability to speak clearly and work alone. For information about volunteer development, please refer to *Recruiting Volunteers*, Crisp Publications.

2. The work space location should be positive to overcome the high degree of rejection a DDC representative receives when compared to the other employees or volunteers. The work area should be private, quiet and comfortable with adequate furniture, light and ventilation.

3. The personal computer should have an optional modem for a dialer and contact management marketing software.

4. The relationship marketing software should have the capacity to store marketing data, customize letters and filter data for reports and database activity results. The software is critical for simplifying donor data tracking and customizing donor correspondence. For information about marketing software, please review the authors' note at the end of the book.

5. The laser or letter quality printer for customized donor correspondence should be easily accessible.

6. The telephone with an optional headset for multiple phone calls should be conveniently installed next to the computer.

STEP 2: ESTABLISH THE DDC DATABASE

The DDC can store raw numerical contribution data and it can compile specific information about individual donors or corporate donors for increased giving.

When planning for the collection of database information, you can collect information about individual donors, corporate donors, and volunteers in one database or you can create separate databases for specific target groups. If you decide to collect information about all groups in one database, the relationship marketing software can be programmed to sort individual accounts with specific characteristics or with a combination of characteristics. Characteristics can include:

- Target population group

- Current level of giving

- Projected level of giving

- Type of business

- Level of community involvement

- Specific areas of interests

- Specific interests in the organization's fund-raising activities

- Specific interests in the organization's program activities

- Specific interests in the organization's volunteer opportunities

- Current participation in the organization

- Anticipated future participation in the organization

For the purpose of this book, it is assumed that one central database will be created for all target groups.

STEP 3: IDENTIFY THE DDC TARGET GROUPS

Donors and corporate donors can be defined as anyone in the community that can donate money, resources or services to your organization. When planning your donor database, consider the following groups for updating and collecting data:

- [ ] Individuals or companies that have previously donated money or resources to your organization
- [ ] Individuals or companies that have requested or received information about your organization
- [ ] Clients and prospective clients
- [ ] Local service and community groups
- [ ] Local merchants
- [ ] Public organizations and employees
- [ ] All related trade or professional associations
- [ ] School, university and college personnel
- [ ] College and trade school students and interns
- [ ] Youth groups
- [ ] Community leaders
- [ ] Labor unions
- [ ] Media leaders
- [ ] Church leaders
- [ ] Senior groups
- [ ] Companies that are committed to community service projects
- [ ] Companies that you purchase services from

Add other groups that your organization could consider as donors:

_____

_____

_____

STEP 4: DETERMINE WHAT INFORMATION IS VALUABLE

When creating your database, you will want to consider types of information that may be valuable to you in developing a donor relationship. You will want to determine who your best donors are so you can spend more time nurturing your relationship with them. You will also want to collect information about the donor that you can use for customized correspondence. Information should be organized for easy classification and report generation. Consider the following pieces of information you want to collect about a donor or corporate donor:

General Questions About the Donor

- Name, address, telephone number, fax number verified

- Donor's occupation or title

- Donor's past relationship with the organization

- Donor's past financial contributions or donations to the organization

- Prospective donor's potential for a financial contribution

- Donor's personality type

- Donor's community service activities

- Donor's human service interests

- Donor's professional affiliations

- Other resources the donor can donate

General Questions About a Corporate Donor

- Company name, address, telephone number, fax number verified

- Type of business or industry

- Company size

- Company contact's name and title

- Decision level of contact

- Company's past relationship with the organization

- Company's past financial contributions or donations to the organization

- Prospective corporate donor's potential for a financial contribution

- Company's present growth factor

- Company's major customers and suppliers

- Company's personality type

- How company policy is communicated to the employees

- Company's desired community profile

- Company's community activities

- Company's health awareness programs

- Contact's perception about the human services that can best benefit the company's employees

- Verify if the company has a social events committee or employee activities committee

- Annual company revenue

- Ask for the company's annual report

HOW TO DETERMINE THE DONOR'S OR CORPORATE CONTACT'S PERSONALITY TYPE

Understanding the donor's or corporate contact's personality type is the key to effective communication. It is also beneficial for you to determine personality type because:

► You can create customized correspondence according to the individual's personality type.

► You can understand the donor's philanthropic personality.

► You will not waste time telling a donor about a giving motive that the donor does not value.

► Your donor will "hear" you.

► Your donor will believe in what you are offering.

When you speak with a donor or corporate contact pay attention to the following:

- During the first thirty seconds of a phone conversation decide if the tone of the person's voice expresses feelings or is flat.

- Determine whether the person on the phone is asserting and communicates directly or is non-asserting and asks questions. With this information you can determine the speaker's personality.

- If the donor is expressive and communicates directly, the donor demonstrates an "expressive" personality.

- If the donor is expressive and asks questions, the donor demonstrates an "amiable" personality.

- If the donor's voice is flat and communicates directly, the donor demonstrates a "bold" personality.

- If the donor's voice is flat and asks questions, the donor demonstrates an "analytical" personality.

After determining the donor's personality type, review the personality type charts on the following pages. A corporate contact's personality type tends to represent the company's personality type nearly 80 percent of the time.

Checklist to Identify Telephone Personalities

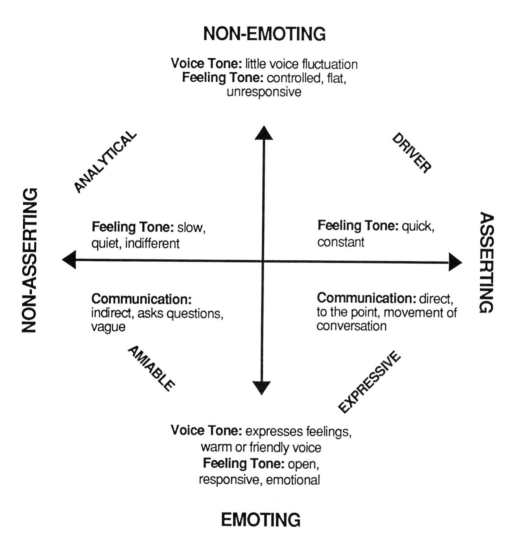

NON-EMOTING

Voice Tone: little voice fluctuation
Feeling Tone: controlled, flat,
unresponsive

ANALYTICAL

DRIVER

NON-ASSERTING

ASSERTING

Feeling Tone: slow,
quiet, indifferent

Feeling Tone: quick,
constant

Communication:
indirect, asks questions,
vague

Communication: direct,
to the point, movement of
conversation

AMIABLE

EXPRESSIVE

Voice Tone: expresses feelings,
warm or friendly voice
Feeling Tone: open,
responsive, emotional

EMOTING

Contribution Motives of Personality Types

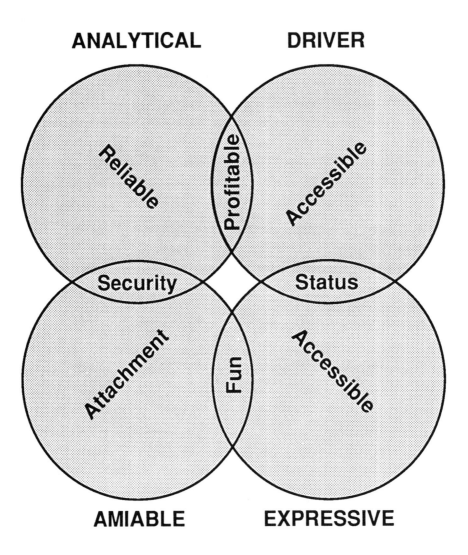

ANALYTICAL   DRIVER

Reliable   Profitable   Accessible

Security   Status

Attachment   Fun   Accessible

AMIABLE   EXPRESSIVE

The donor will be motivated to contribute to your organization when:

1. You convincingly present a need.

2. You identify the donor's contribution motives.

3. You satisfy the donor's criteria for giving.

How to Design a Survey to Collect Database Information

After identifying the data you want to store in your database, design a donor or corporate donor multiple choice information survey for computer entry. Marketing software programs have the capacity to:

1. Program preselected questions

2. Program preselected answers to questions

3. Sort data by a specific characteristic

4. Sort data by a combination of characteristics

5. Compile sorted data in computer generated reports

6. Track daily activities

7. Summarize daily database activities in a computer generated report

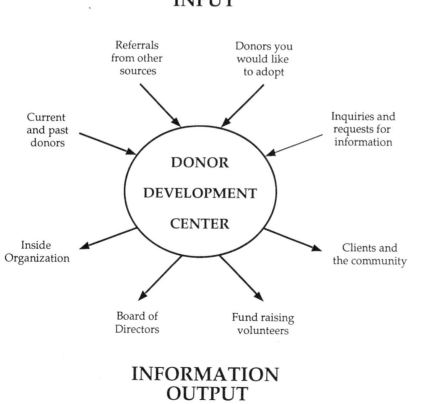

INFORMATION INPUT

Referrals from other sources

Donors you would like to adopt

Current and past donors

Inquiries and requests for information

DONOR DEVELOPMENT CENTER

Inside Organization

Clients and the community

Board of Directors

Fund raising volunteers

INFORMATION OUTPUT

SAMPLE DONOR'S DATABASE SURVEY

Donor's name _____ Phone _____

Address _____ Fax phone _____

City, state _____ Zip, country _____

Company name _____ Employment title _____

Please check the information that most closely matches the company's answer:

1. Type of employment

___ Agricultural	___ Real Estate	___ Construction
___ Computers	___ Medical	___ Insurance
___ Public Utilities	___ Manufacturing	___ Legal
___ Hotels	___ Retail	___ Other
___ Food	___ Schools	_____
___ Finance	___ Entertainment	_____

2. Donor's past relationship with organization

___ Financial donor	___ Donated resources
___ Donated labor	___ Past prospect
___ Referral	___ Activity sponsor

3. Estimated value of donor's financial contributions and donations during the last year

___ Less than $50	___ $250–$500
___ $50–$100	___ $500–$1,000
___ $100–$250	___ $1,000+

4. Potential for future increased giving

___ High	___ Average
___ Low	___ Negative

SAMPLE CORPORATE DONOR DATABASE SURVEY

Company name _____ Phone _____

Address _____ Fax phone _____

City, state _____ Zip, country _____

Contact's name _____ Contact's title _____

Please check the information that most closely matches the company's answer:

1. Type of business or industry

   ___ Agricultural   ___ Real Estate   ___ Construction
   ___ Computers   ___ Medical   ___ Insurance
   ___ Public Utilities   ___ Manufacturing   ___ Legal
   ___ Hotels   ___ Retail   ___ Other
   ___ Food   ___ Schools   _____
   ___ Finance   ___ Entertainment   _____

2. Company size

   ___ 1–25   ___ 200–500
   ___ 26–50   ___ 501–1000
   ___ 51–100   ___ 1000–2500
   ___ 101–200   ___ 2501+

3. Decision level of contact

   ___ Decision maker   ___ Decision influencer
   ___ Information collector   ___ Screener

4. Company's past relationship with organization

   ___ Financial donor   ___ Donated resources
   ___ Donated labor   ___ Past prospect
   ___ Referral   ___ Activity sponsor

CREATE YOUR OWN DATABASE SURVEY

Review the lists of information questions for creating a database. In the spaces provided list ten donor or corporate donor information questions you want to know about. Create four probable responses after each question.

Question #1: _____

Responses: _____

_____

_____

Question #2: _____

Responses: _____

_____

_____

Question #3: _____

Responses: _____

_____

_____

Question #4: _____

Responses: _____

_____

_____

Question #5: _____

Responses: _____

_____

_____

Question #6: _____

Responses: _____

_____

_____

Question #7: _____

Responses: _____

_____

_____

Question #8: _____

Responses: _____

_____

_____

Question #9: _____

Responses: _____

_____

_____

Question #10: _____

Responses: _____

_____

_____

Additional information to be entered into the database: _____

_____

_____

STEP 5: STRATEGIES FOR COLLECTING INFORMATION

Once you have designed your database survey, you can collect the survey responses through:

► Telephone interviews

► Mail surveys

► In person after receiving a contribution

Telephone interviews can be most effective when you take the time to create a phone format script. The script should include:

► An introduction

► A benefit statement (See page 71 for a benefit statement definition)

► An explanation about the survey

► A determination about the donor's present needs

After completing the survey, you can mail additional information to the donor or corporate donor. The next few pages include donor and corporate donor phone format work sheets, strategies for telephone use, priority and message-specific correspondence samples.

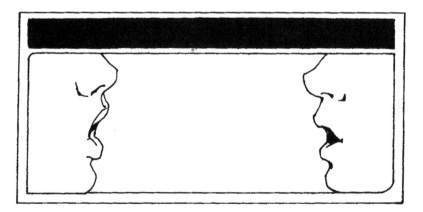

DONOR'S CONFIRMING STRATEGY
PHONE FORMAT

Introduction:

_____

_____

_____

Benefit statement:

_____

_____

_____

Database questions:

_____

_____

_____

Explanation of why you are calling:

_____

_____

_____

Ask about the donor's present needs, especially:

_____

_____

_____

During the thank-you phase:

- Tell the donor to watch for your letter that will explain more about the organization's services and about the benefits that can be received from the Donor Development Center.

- Thank the donor for his or her time.

CORPORATE DONOR'S CONFIRMING STRATEGY PHONE FORMAT

Introduction:

_____

_____

_____

Benefit statement:

_____

_____

_____

Confirm:

• Address
• Main telephone number
• All other facts that need to be confirmed

_____

_____

_____

Request:

• Fax number
• Decision maker's name
• Answers to database questions

_____

_____

_____

Before terminating the conversation:

• Ask for the person's name.
• Thank the person for his or her time.
• Tell the person to phone you for any further information.

DONOR DEVELOPMENT CENTER TELEPHONE COURTESY

Consider the following telephone courtesy skills before contacting donors about database information or contributions.

► Speak with a smile and enthusiasm when talking on the phone.

► Use the donor's name at least three times within the first few seconds of the phone conversation.

► Never eat or drink while on the phone.

► Always ask if you can put a donor on hold and use the hold button whenever you leave the phone.

► Respect the donor's sense of urgency.

► Avoid slang and poor grammar.

► Never interrupt and carefully listen to the donor's feelings and thoughts.

► Tie emotion to your voice as you visualize who you are talking to.

► Limit your own talking.

► Listen to the donor's speech patterns and respond to the donor using the same kind of speech patterns.

► Consider the importance of voice mirroring and matching.

► Ask clarifying questions if you don't understand what has been said.

► Ask open-ended questions that start with who, what, where, when, why or how to gain additional information.

► Do not shift a donor's complaint onto someone else without an explanation.

► Never transfer a frustrated donor to an unsuspecting co-worker.

► Remain courteous and considerate at all times. It's not what you say, it's how you say it.

PHONE FORMAT
INTRODUCTION WORKSHEET

1. Did you use the donor's name two or three times at the beginning of the conversation?

_____

_____

_____

2. Did you introduce yourself and identify your organization's relationship to the donor? Did you ask if the donor had a few minutes to talk?

_____

_____

_____

3. Did you tell donor which organization you were calling from and why you were calling?

_____

_____

HOW TO OVERCOME TELEPHONE SCREENING AND COMPLETE THE TELEPHONE CALL

Telephone screening occurs when a donor or corporate decision maker only has limited time available and instructs the secretary to forward important phone calls only. Consider the following guidelines to overcome telephone screening:

- Plan before making each phone call. Know as much information as possible about the donor and develop a plan of what you need to know.

- Create a rapport with the screener. Ask for help, explain why you need to get through and expect to be successful.

- Review the basic telephone courtesy guidelines and never make an enemy of the screener.

- Use the donor's or decision maker's first name when asking to speak with him or her.

- Use the receptionist's or secretary's first name.

- Use a friendly and expecting-to-be-transferred voice.

- Use your organization's name if the organization is important to the donor.

- Maintain control throughout the phone call.

- Call before or after business hours or at noon.

- Break the rule of not telling the screener who you are. Tell the screener about all of the benefits of why you should be transferred to the donor or decision maker and ask for help.

- Identify available times and set a time to retry the phone call.

- Make yourself available and establish times that you are available.

- Know when to quit. When all else fails, write the donor or decision maker a letter, ask for a return phone call, and delete the record if there is no response.

IMPLEMENTING SEGMENTATION AND PRIORITY STRATEGIES

Segmentation and priority strategies help you prioritize your time for donors according to their greatest giving potential. The strategies also can assist you in developing message-specific correspondence for various donor segments.

You can implement donor and corporate donor segmentation and priority strategies once you start collecting database information about a group of donors. Your donors and corporate donors can be segmented and prioritized by:

✔ Human service interest

✔ Type of community service commitments and contributions

✔ Type of business or profession

✔ Services the donor can provide your organization

✔ Past relationship with the organization

✔ Past financial contributions or donations to the organization

✔ Professional affiliations

✔ Personality type and corporate culture

✔ Desired community profile

✔ Prospect level

Consider your organization's donors and corporate donors. In the spaces provided identify five ways you can prioritize and segment your donors according to the information you have collected about them.

1. _____

2. _____

3. _____

4. _____

5. _____

Creating Message-Specific Correspondence with Benefit Statements

You can create message-specific correspondence for each donor and corporate donor segment. Consider the following when developing message-specific correspondence:

- What is the personality type or corporate culture of the donor segment?

- What do you want to communicate to this donor segment?

- How will donating to your cause benefit the donor?

- When or how often do you want to communicate this message to the group?

- Where do you plan to send the communication?

- What type of correspondence do you plan to use for this donor segment?

Benefit Statements

Benefit statements are a critical component of message-specific correspondence and verbal communication. Benefit statements tell the donor what services the organization can provide the donor in exchange for a contribution. Examples can include:

- The donor will receive a free cholesterol test when he or she contributes $100 or more to the organization.

- The donor will receive a free stress reduction book when contributing $50 or more to the organization.

- The corporate donor will receive free assistance in organizing a wellness class for the employees when contributing $1,000 or more.

CUSTOMIZED MAILER WORKSHEET

Once you have identified your donor segment, the message you want to communicate and how you want to communicate the message, plan and design a customized correspondence mailer in the spaces provided.

1. Segment Group Characteristics: _____

_____

_____

_____

2. Message Goals: _____

_____

_____

_____

3. Projected Date for Initial Mailing: _____

4. Follow-up Mailing Dates: _____

5. Home or Office Mailing: _____

6. Circle the Donor Segment's Overall Personality Type:

Analytical   Amiable   Bold   Expressive

7. Overall Human Service Interest: _____

_____

_____

8. Circle the Donor Segment's Prospect Level:

High   Medium   Low   Negative

9. Customized Benefit Statement for this Donor Segment: _____

_____

_____

_____

_____

_____

_____

Now you can create and mail your customized mailer for this donor segment.

PLANNING YOUR DONOR DEVELOPMENT CAMPAIGN

You can plan your donor development campaign after you:

1. Identify the donors

2. Create a donor development information survey

3. Determine how to communicate effectively with different donor personality types on the phone or by mail

The donor development campaign is a system of predetermined activities to:

- Collect database information

- Create leads for new donors

- Educate the donor about your services

- Educate the donor about social services in the community

- Nurture a relationship with the donor

- Solicit financial contributions

- Solicit labor support and other donations

The DDC campaign may include some or all of the following activities:

- Systematic phone calls

- Customized personal letters

- Informational brochures, newsletters, and articles about your services or related social services in your community

- Fax transmittals

- In-person call by volunteer

On the following page create a sample donor development campaign for your organization.

SAMPLE PLAN FOR A DONOR DEVELOPMENT CAMPAIGN

List two goals and four objectives for your campaign in the spaces provided.

Donor Development Campaign Goal #1:

_____

_____

First Objective: _____

_____

Second Objective: _____

_____

Donor Development Campaign Goal #2:

_____

_____

First Objective: _____

_____

Second Objective: _____

_____

Activity Plan to Support the Proposed Goals and Objectives

Planned Activity	Activity Dates	Results

HOW TO CREATE MAILERS FOR THE CAMPAIGN

You can create the following types of direct mail materials for your donor or corporate donor campaign:

High-impact mailers should include:

1. A unique personal letter explaining your reasons for contacting the donor or corporate donor and the benefits to the donor or corporate donor

2. Suggested donations

3. A product related to your organization offered as a ''premium'' for a minimum (but high) donation.

Mid-impact mailers can include:

1. A personalized form letter that explains benefits to the donor or corporate donor

2. Suggested donations

3. A premium offer for a minimum donation

Low-impact mailers might include:

1. A personalized form letter of explanation

2. Suggested donations

Consider the donor's or corporate donor contact's personality type and perceived areas of social service interests when creating customized mail materials. A letter to an analytical donor would include numerical facts whereas a letter to an expressive donor can be warm and folksy.

Before phoning your donors or corporate donors, create thank-you form letters considering the four different personality types and different services your organization provides. You will also need to create a form letter for prospective donors or donors who do not want to talk with you. Always follow up a telephone conversation with a personalized mailer. Test each newly developed personalized form letter for effectiveness and make adjustments as necessary.

THANK-YOU LETTER

Below is a sample thank-you letter to an analytical personality type donor interested in affordable health care.

```
Savings Health Clinic
1122 Safety Court
Hopeland, OK 22334

Mr. Ross Best
15 Caring Dr.
Hopeland, OK 22334

Dear Ross,

As the Donor Development Coordinator for Savings Health Clinic, my
primary responsibility is to verify information about you so that we
can identify specific ways our organization can meet your needs.

Savings Health Clinic strives to respond reliably to the health care
needs of uninsured or under-insured patients. In 1992 it cost the
county $30 million to provide health care to uninsured patients. Last
year our agency allocated $414,897 to provide community care, health
education and health counseling to 1,287 county residents.

Because of your interest in quality health prevention, we have
enclosed a coupon for a discount cholesterol test and a brochure
describing the various services our programs provide. Additionally,
I have included a description of the eight different ways you can
contribute to our programs.

Thank you for your commitment to quality and responsiveness. We look
forward to talking with you next week.

Sincerely,



Mary Lou Abele
Donor Development Coordinator

P.S. I enjoyed hearing about your mother's success with our senior
     nutrition program.
```

THANK-YOU LETTER (continued)

Below is a sample thank-you letter to an analytical personality type corporate donor contact interested in affordable health care.

Savings Health Clinic
1122 Safety Court
Hopeland, OK 22334

Mr. John Ready
President
We Care Parcel Service
100 Pare Dr.
Hopeland, OK 22334

Dear Mr. Ready,

As the Donor Development Coordinator for Savings Health Clinic, my primary responsibility is to verify information about you so that we can identify specific ways our organization can meet your needs.

Savings Health Clinic strives to respond reliably to the health care needs of uninsured or under-insured patients. In 1992 it cost the county $30 million to provide health care to uninsured patients. Last year our agency allocated $414,897 to provide community care, health education and health counseling to 1,287 county residents.

Because of your company's interest in quality health prevention, we have enclosed our stress reduction employee guide and a brochure describing the various services our programs provide. Additionally, I have included a description of the eight different ways you can contribute to our programs.

Thank you for your commitment to quality and responsiveness. We look forward to talking with you next week.

Sincerely,

Mary Lou Abele
Donor Development Coordinator

P.S. I enjoyed hearing about your company's success in reducing job-related injuries.

SAMPLE THANK-YOU LETTER WORKSHEET

Circle the personality type of the donor or corporate donor contact.

Analytical   Bold   Amiable   Expressive

Circle the donor's or corporate donor's perceived human service interest.

Health care   Dental care   Parent education   AIDS

Introduction and personal explanation of why you are contacting the donor or corporate donor:

_____

_____

_____

_____

Explanation of the benefits to the donor or corporate donor:

_____

_____

_____

_____

An offer to the donor or corporate donor:

_____

_____

Something of value for the donor or corporate donor:

_____

_____

HOW TO DESIGN THE CAMPAIGN CALL

Campaign calls include the following activities:

- An introduction and a personal explanation of why you are contacting the donor

- An explanation of the benefits to the donor

- Promotional campaign questions

- Database questions

- Thank you

Before initiating a phone call, review the following guidelines for success:

1. Establish a confident attitude and be clear about the purpose for the call.

2. Start with an introduction and use the donor's name two or three times at the beginning of the conversation.

3. Ask if the donor has time to talk and tell the donor what organization you are calling from.

4. Develop a benefit statement.

5. During the questioning phase, ask questions that will help you understand the donor's needs and personality type.

6. Explain that you are calling to tell the donor about the organization's new Donor Development Center and about the resulting benefits to the donor.

7. Give the donor your name and phone number so that the donor can reach you when assistance is needed.

8. Ask about the donor's present needs.

9. Ask the donor to watch for a letter from you that will tell more about the organization's services and the Donor Development Center.

10. Thank the donor for his or her time and hang up.

11. After the phone call, update your database records and send your personalized form letter.

DEVELOPING CUSTOMIZED CAMPAIGNS

You can develop customized campaigns for donor and corporate donor segments by creating a unique mix of activities to support the needs of a particular segment group. Consider the following examples of how various organizations customized their donor campaigns to meet the needs of individual donor segments:

Example 1:

Friends Alliance provides transitional housing, case management, and counseling to severely emotionally disturbed adults. Historically the organization receives financial donations from the clients' families and friends. The organization decided to recruit new donors by presenting community speeches and by developing mailers about mental health resources and support systems. After a community member attends a speech, the person's name is entered into the donor database for a thank-you phone call and for further correspondence.

Example 2:

Learning Disabilities Supporters provides learning disability information and support services to families of children with learning disabilities. The organization receives most of its funding through family contributions. The organization has recently expanded its donors by presenting learning disability information nights at local schools. Families that attend the presentation can learn how to detect possible learning handicaps in family members. Donor families are offered additional seminars about ways parents can help their children succeed in school and in the community.

Example 3:

Community Cares is a nonprofit service group of professionals who want to provide support services to their community. The organization's service projects are funded by annual fees collected from each member. The group has decided to increase its membership by organizing monthly community human service resource forums. Community members that attend the meetings are later recruited to join the organization as either a member or a contributing member.

CUSTOMIZED CAMPAIGN WORKSHEET

Review the previously described customized campaign examples and consider your current donor segments. In the spaces provided create a customized campaign strategy for one of your donor segments.

Describe the donor segment's leading characteristics.

_____

_____

_____

What is the donor segment's overall past relationship with your organization?

_____

_____

_____

What service can your organization provide to the donor segment to enhance the present level of contributions?

_____

_____

_____

What service can your organization provide to recruit new donors?

_____

_____

_____

What ongoing benefits will your organization offer the donor segment to increase future contributions?

_____

_____

_____

REPORTING AND TRACKING DAILY ACTIVITIES

You can track and report daily activities automatically when using the automatic dialer feature offered in various marketing relationship software packages. Most marketing relationship software packages also have the capability to compile and generate daily, weekly and monthly reports on up to five segment characteristics. Examples include:

► A corporate donor's prospect report that lists the company's name, generalized size, growth potential and prospect contribution level.

► A report totaling each different multiple choice donor response in the database. Examples include the total number of donors and prospect donors with bold personalities or the total number of donors that work in manufacturing.

► A donor report that lists the donor's name, occupation or general business, past contributions average, level of community service and human service area of interest.

In the spaces provided list five different activity reports that would benefit your organization.

1. _____

   _____

2. _____

   _____

3. _____

   _____

4. _____

   _____

5. _____

   _____

SECTION

5

Planned Giving and
Charitable Trusts

PLANNED GIVING AND CHARITABLE TRUSTS

Planned giving is the process of donating and transferring property or other assets to a nonprofit organization through a charitable trust. The benefits to the donor include:

▶ The donor is offered a method for donating a significant asset to a worthy cause and can receive income from the donated asset.

▶ The donor can receive a tax deduction from the donated asset.

▶ Money can be left to the donor's heirs equal to or greater than the original asset's value.

Nonprofits should encourage planned giving because the organization can receive substantial long-term contributions from dedicated donors. Although there are many different types of charitable trusts, the two most common are the charitable remainder trust and the charitable remainder untrust. The major difference between these two is the income pay out process to the donor.

Before entering into any planned giving charitable trust agreement with a donor, consult an accountant and an attorney. Planned giving regulations are very specific and require qualified assistance to insure compliance.

The following donor groups should be approached about planned giving:

1. The top 20 percent of your contributors

2. Donors with assets that are fully paid for and with assets that have greatly appreciated in value

3. Donors with fully paid-for assets that are concerned about having sufficient income for retirement

4. High net-worth contributors that are interested in donating to a nonprofit

5. New contributors who have not determined a fixed method of giving

THE BASIC STEPS FOR ESTABLISHING A CHARITABLE TRUST

 STEP 1   Assets are donated by the giver to the nonprofit organization through a charitable trust.

 STEP 2   The charitable trust sells the asset and invests the proceeds. Capital gains tax does not need to be paid by the donor or the organization.

 STEP 3   The donor receives a charitable tax deduction, a lifetime income from the sale of asset investment and an opportunity to give a significant contribution to a worthy cause.

 STEP 4   The donor's heirs can receive a tax-free inheritance with an additional insurance trust.

STEP 5   The nonprofit receives the full amount of the donation upon the death of the donor.

Charitable Trust Case Study

DONOR'S ASSET:	Real estate property currently valued at $275,000 with an original investment of $15,000
TAX BRACKET:	35%
DESIRED RETURN ON INVESTMENT:	11%
ESTIMATED DURATION OF RETURN:	27 YEARS

Example when the donor sells the asset, pays taxes, invests money and lives off the invested income:

The donor will pay approximately $91,000 in taxes after selling the $275,000 asset and will invest the remaining capital to receive a lifetime income of $546,000. When the donor dies, his estate will be valued at $184,000 with no proceeds allocated to his favorite charity.

   Total Pay Out = $733,000

Example when a charitable trust is used as a vehicle by the donor to contribute to a charity:

The annual 7 percent pay out to the donor is not taxed. The donor will receive a lifetime income of $906,000. When the donor dies, the estate will receive nothing and the nonprofit will receive $762,000.

   Total Pay Out = $1,668,000

Example when a charitable trust plus insurance trust is used as a vehicle to give to the charity and to the estate heirs:

The lifetime cost of the donor's life insurance is $56,000. The value of the policy is $500,000 with no taxes paid. The donor will receive $850,000 as a lifetime income. The heirs to the donor's estate will receive $500,000 and the nonprofit organization will receive $762,000.

   Total Pay Out = $2,112,000

CHARITABLE TRUST WORKSHEET

This worksheet can help donors evaluate the feasibility of creating a charitable trust. A professional opinion should be obtained before a final decision is made.

Value of asset to be donated   (1) _____

Annual percentage of pay out desired on
donated asset   (2) _____

Estimated life expectancy   (3) _____

Total pay out (Line 2 × Line 1 × Line 3)   (4) _____

Amount of pay out from investment if asset is
sold on the open market, taxes are paid, and
principle is invested. (These figures are
estimates. Formula is the same as above with
the exception of amount of taxes paid on the
sale of the asset.)   (5) _____

Total pay out   (6) _____

Total monetary benefit of charitable trust
(Line 4 − Line 5)   (7) _____

Value of estate to be left   (8) _____

Total cost of insurance to fund estate   (9) _____

New total pay out to donor (total pay out less
total cost of insurance)   (10) _____

Soliciting for Other Types of Donations

SOLICITING FOR OTHER TYPES OF DONATIONS

Financial donations are valuable for an organization's:

- Day-to-day operations
- Management and general expenses
- Program services
- Capital expenditures
- Future goals

An organization should not limit its donation solicitations to only money because many donors and companies prefer to donate other types of resources to an organization.

Consider the following examples of multiple-resource donations:

Example 1: *Women's and Children's Shelter for Victims of Domestic Violence*

The Women's Shelter has always encouraged a diversity of donations for its displaced clients. The shelter recruits volunteers for support counseling, child care, legal guidance, medical services and family education. Local merchants donate food, clothing, sample toiletries, toys, household goods, furniture and maintenance services. Community members also donate clothing, toys and household items. Local restaurants provide the mothers and children with meal coupons.

Example 2: *After-School Youth Program*

The After-School Youth Program operates out of a local church gym. Neighborhood restaurants donate food for afternoon snacks. Computers are provided by local computer companies for tutorial and recreational use. Community organizations provide on-site sports activities. The local library offers a weekly story hour and community college students provide tutoring services at the site.

List the resources that are donated to a human service program in your community.

_____

_____

You will discover how to solicit multiple resources for your organization in the next section.

EQUIPMENT DONATIONS

Equipment donations can benefit your organization when:

- A need for the donation has been identified

- The need has been identified in a master plan

- Your organization is flexible about receiving unplanned equipment

- You are prepared to negotiate for other equipment options

- You can offer the donor a benefit for the donation

- You recognize the donor for the contribution

- You encourage and nurture an ongoing relationship

- You provide the donor with resources that can benefit him or her

- You empower the donor to expand and diversify his or her giving

List ten types of equipment donations that can benefit your organization or enhance your delivery of services.

1. _____

2. _____

3. _____

4. _____

5. _____

6. _____

7. _____

8. _____

9. _____

10. _____

List six donors or merchants you can approach for equipment.

1. _____   2. _____

3. _____   4. _____

5. _____   6. _____

What is your benefit statement and how will you recognize the donor for the contribution?

_____

_____

_____

_____

_____

_____

_____

_____

IN-KIND SERVICES

In-kind services can be provided by a variety of sources to meet the management, program and operational needs of your organization. Volunteers and service contractors can donate the following organization services:

✔ Financial accounting and bookkeeping

✔ Legal counsel

✔ Fund-raising

✔ Advertising and public relations

✔ Staff training

✔ Clerical support

✔ Facility maintenance

✔ Facility use

✔ Equipment use

✔ Food services

✔ Transportation

✔ Program volunteers

Consider your current use of volunteers and the community for supporting your organization's activities. List the in-kind services your organization receives.

_____

_____

_____

List five services your organization can receive through in-kind services and identify who can provide the services.

1. Service: _____ Provider: _____

2. Service: _____ Provider: _____

3. Service: _____ Provider: _____

4. Service: _____ Provider: _____

5. Service: _____ Provider: _____

DISCOUNT COUPONS

All services and product prices can be negotiated. Many sellers do not like to donate, but prefer to offer service and product discounts or discount coupons. Nonprofits can buy products and services for reduced prices through merchant and service provider discount coupons. Additional benefits for the buyer and seller include:

- The seller is more likely to get your service when offering a discount.

- Discount coupons encourage your ongoing business commitment.

- The buyer and seller relationship is nurtured through ongoing transactions.

- The buyer and seller can continually adjust the negotiated agreement.

- The seller can receive free promotional support from you.

- The seller can receive program services from you.

- The seller can become a resource.

- The seller can become a financial donor.

- The seller can become an organization volunteer.

List three community contacts that can provide discount coupons to your organization.

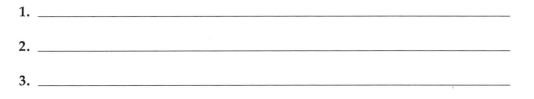

1. _____

2. _____

3. _____

List three benefits your organization can offer the discount coupon providers.

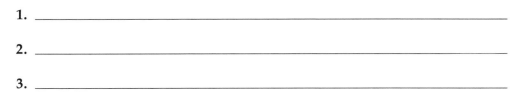

1. _____

2. _____

3. _____

FOOD AND SUPPLIES FOR EVENTS

Planning special events offers ample solicitation opportunities. Consider the following special event example:

Community Cares is planning its annual fund-raising dinner. The organization's event donations include:

- Rosalinda's Casa will cater the dinner
- Gonzalez Brothers will provide entertainment
- Fernando's Fiesta Supply is contributing decorations
- Robledo's Nursery will create table centerpieces
- Gomez Originals will design the dinner programs
- Francisco Studio will photograph guests
- *The Heart Times* will provide free advertising and press coverage
- Lee's Cleaning will provide janitorial support

Consider the next special event your organization is planning. Identify six services that can be donated or discounted for the event and list prospective community donors for the service.

1. Service: _____ Donor: _____

2. Service: _____ Donor: _____

3. Service: _____ Donor: _____

4. Service: _____ Donor: _____

5. Service: _____ Donor: _____

6. Service: _____ Donor: _____

What benefits will you offer the donors?

_____

_____

_____

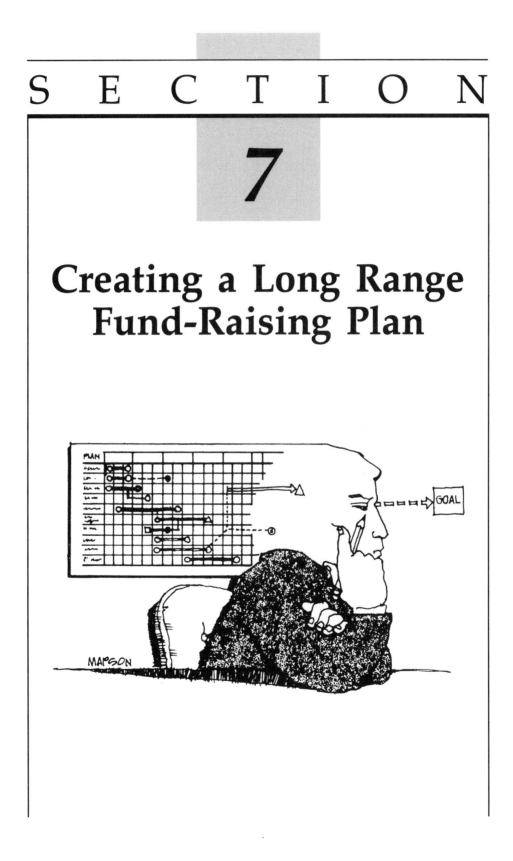

SECTION

7

Creating a Long Range Fund-Raising Plan

CREATING A LONG RANGE FUND-RAISING PLAN

Creating an effective long range fund-raising plan requires patience, vision and resources. Answer the following questions about your organization. Then ask these questions of others who hear you talk about your organization or have had some contact with your services.

► What fund-raising activities stand out most when you think about your organization?

► What fund-raising activity do I elaborate on when I talk about my organization?

► What really excites me about my organization's fund-raising activities?

► What frustrates me the most about my organization's fund-raising activities?

► What successful fund-raising activities have I attended in the community?

► What did I appreciate most about the events?

► If there were no time or resource limits, what fund-raising events would I like to plan for my organization?

► What unlimited resources would I need to fulfill this dream?

► What are my community's greatest assets?

► How can my organization best utilize the community's assets in a fund-raising activity?

► What are my community's greatest limitations?

► How can my organization overcome the community's limitations when fund-raising?

► What are my greatest fund-raising achievements?

► How can I capitalize on these when fund-raising?

► What have I learned about myself from these questions?

► What have I learned about my organization from these questions?

OVERALL STRATEGIES

Review your answers to the previous questions and consider the various fund-raising activities described in this book. List two fund-raising activities that you want to develop for your organization in the next year. Identify when the event will take place and when the supporting activities will need to be accomplished. Also determine how you will evaluate the progress or effectiveness of the fund-raising strategy.

Fund-Raising Activity #1: _____

Date for Activity: _____

Supporting Activities	Time	Evaluation
_____	_____	_____
_____	_____	_____
_____	_____	_____
_____	_____	_____

List two supplementary fund-raising activities you can build into this strategy next year.

1. _____

2. _____

Fund-Raising Activity #2: _____

Date for Activity: _____

Supporting Activities	Time	Evaluation
_____	_____	_____
_____	_____	_____
_____	_____	_____
_____	_____	_____

List two supplementary fund-raising activities you can build into this strategy next year.

1. _____

2. _____

Review your answers and identify three future fund-raising strategies for your organization.

DELEGATION OF RESPONSIBILITIES

Planning fund-raising activities is overwhelming when considering the amount of staff labor that is required to organize an activity. Job assignments can be modified to include volunteers within your organization. Additional volunteers can be recruited for specific fund-raising needs.

Review the first fund-raising activity you want to develop for your organization in the next year. Determine who will be responsible for each planning segment.

Fund-Raising Activity: _____

Planning Committee _____

_____

_____

_____

Publicity _____

_____

Printing and Duplicating _____

Community Donations _____

_____

Accounting Support _____

Legal Support _____

Facility Support _____

Custodial _____

Decorating _____

Database Entry of Guests _____

Other _____

_____

When reviewing the activity job responsibilities, what responsibilities still need additional labor support?

How do you plan to recruit volunteers to respond to these needs?

SECTION

8

The Creative Utilization of Resources

THE CREATIVE UTILIZATION OF RESOURCES

As your organization develops new fund-raising relationships with donors and the community, ongoing organization resource evaluations and adjustments are essential. Community resources are your most precious resource. They must be creatively shared with other groups to meet the community's multiple human service needs. This, or a similar form, should be used as part of an ongoing evaluation process.

Shared Resource Evaluation Form

Circle the appropriate numerical value for each item.

		Low			High	
1.	The organization shares its resources	1	2	3	4	5
2.	The organization shares its staff	1	2	3	4	5
3.	The organization shares its volunteers	1	2	3	4	5
4.	The organization shares its facility	1	2	3	4	5
5.	The organization shares its equipment	1	2	3	4	5
6.	The organization shares training opportunities	1	2	3	4	5
7.	The organization shares media contacts	1	2	3	4	5
8.	The organization shares technical expertise	1	2	3	4	5
9.	The organization shares custodial services	1	2	3	4	5
10.	The organization shares donations	1	2	3	4	5
11.	The organization shares publications	1	2	3	4	5
12.	The organization collaborates for grants	1	2	3	4	5
13.	The organization shares direct mail campaigns	1	2	3	4	5
14.	The organization shares its donor database	1	2	3	4	5
15.	The organization shares special events	1	2	3	4	5
16.	The organization shares planned giving efforts	1	2	3	4	5
17.	The organization plans for collaborations	1	2	3	4	5
18.	The organization cross-trains its volunteers	1	2	3	4	5
19.	The organization lives for the future	1	2	3	4	5
20.	The organization is innovative	1	2	3	4	5

Shared Resource Evaluation Form (continued)

Comments on the highest scoring characteristics:

_____

_____

_____

Comments on the lowest scoring characteristics:

_____

_____

_____

Based upon your responses to this evaluation, discuss how your organization is sharing its resources to respond to its community, its employees, its donors and its volunteers:

_____

_____

_____

_____

Review your answers. Which shared resource areas does your organization need to further develop?

_____

_____

_____

What is your plan for action?

_____

_____

_____

In the next few pages you can consider how to creatively utilize people, contacts, facilities and supplies to collaboratively respond to your community needs.

PEOPLE AS A COMMUNITY RESOURCE

People are the bloodline to your organization's success, so they should be nurtured and appropriately utilized. Each community member brings his or her own unique history, talents and skills to your organization. Identifying and capitalizing on each person's skills, talents and resources will enhance your relationship with the community member and will enhance his or her relationship with your organization and the community.

As you read the following case study, decide how you would creatively utilize Sharon's commitment, talents and technical expertise.

Case Study

Sharon, the Community Volunteer

Sharon has always been interested in serving her community. After losing her job as a bookkeeper in a manufacturing facility, Sharon decided to volunteer at the local food bank. Soon she became disillusioned when she found that much of her bookkeeping efforts were not being maintained by staff.

After several months, Sharon decided to work as an independent contractor for a technical writer. She soon became enthusiastic about desktop publishing and returned to school for training. After completing her training, Sharon continues to work as an independent contractor and donates her desktop publishing skills to people who will acknowledge her work.

1. How could the food bank better utilize Sharon's skills?

   _____

   _____

2. How could the food bank evaluate Sharon's interests and assist her in developing new skills?

   _____

   _____

3. What was Sharon's net worth to the food bank when considering the cost of paying a bookkeeper?

   _____

4. What benefits can a nonprofit provide Sharon for her skills?

   _____

CONTACTS AS A COMMUNITY RESOURCE

Networking and building community contacts is essential for an organization's growth and survival. Networking can:

- Introduce the organization to new funding sources
- Introduce the organization to prospective donors
- Introduce the organization to donation sources
- Introduce the organization to technical experts
- Introduce the organization to collaborations
- Introduce the organization to your community

List six neighbors you know. Next to each neighbor's name list a resource or skill that each person can contribute to your organization.

Neighbor's Name	Resource or Skill
1. _____	_____
2. _____	_____
3. _____	_____
4. _____	_____
5. _____	_____
6. _____	_____

Review your list of neighborhood contacts and list three other people you have met through these neighbors. Next to each name list a skill or resource the person can donate.

1. _____	_____
2. _____	_____
3. _____	_____

Review both lists and determine how you can provide benefits to these contacts in exchange for resource support.

_____

_____

FACILITIES AS A COMMUNITY RESOURCE

Facility space is becoming a challenge as community programs grow in quantity and size. Assessing your community's various facilities can serve as a valuable tool for:

- Strategic planning
- Collaborations
- Program access
- Cost-effective program delivery
- Networking
- Fund-raising
- Donor development
- Getting to know your community

List three public facilities located near your organization and determine how each facility can be used for your programs or administrative support activities.

	Facility	Organization Function
1.	_____	_____
2.	_____	_____
3.	_____	_____

What benefits can your organization provide these facilities for free facility use or for reduced rent?

_____

List three private facilities and identify which organization activities each can support.

	Facility	Organization Function
1.	_____	_____
2.	_____	_____
3.	_____	_____

What benefits can your organization provide these facilities for free facility use or for reduced rent?

_____

SUPPLIES AS A COMMUNITY RESOURCE

Administrative and program supplies are a constant drain on your organization's budget. Developing a network of service and product suppliers can:

- Reduce the organization's day-to-day operations
- Develop donors
- Develop volunteers
- Provide free advertising for suppliers
- Recycle suppliers' unwanted materials
- Provide tax-deduction opportunities
- Nurture a relationship with the community

Consider the following examples of how various companies have provided free supplies to organizations.

▶ Mark's Lumber provides free scrap wood to the nursery school for art projects.

▶ Eric's Deli donates day-old bread to the homeless shelter.

▶ Reesa Printing Inc. donates paper scraps to the elementary school.

▶ Soursa Electronics donates obsolete computer supplies to the community's job retraining program.

▶ Leong's Drugs provides personal care samples to the domestic violence shelter.

List three suppliers that you can approach for donations.

	Supplier	Free Supplies
1.	_____	_____
2.	_____	_____
3.	_____	_____

The resource worksheets in this section have demonstrated that fund-raising is not just raising money. It is raising community awareness and a commitment for creatively utilizing the community's resources. Kudos to all that invest and give back to their community.

Contact Management Software

Personal computers and software can help the small, minimally funded nonprofit survive fund-raising. Contact management software is now available for low-cost and high-impact donor development.

Initially contact management marketing software was sold as telemarketing software. It is now an integral part of all high-productivity sales organizations. Effective and economical donor development cannot be accomplished without this type of process. Good contact management software provides support in the following areas:

Complete Contact Management
Simple and Efficient Relationship Management
Flexible Database Management
Complete Reporting Capability

There are several effective contact management marketing software programs currently available. The authors have found that a customized version of TELEMAGIC, by Remote Control of Carlsbad, California, works best for their donor development requirements.

Further information on TELEMAGIC software may be obtained from the above manufacturer or from:

CARL LILJENSTOLPE
PROFIT TECHNOLOGY
LOS GATOS, CALIFORNIA 95030
PHONE 408–866–4990
FAX 408–866–4718

It is not essential to use TELEMAGIC as the donor development software of choice. It is more important to use the contact management software program best suited to your donor development efforts.

NOTES

FOR OTHER FIFTY-MINUTE SELF-STUDY BOOKS
SEE THE BACK OF THIS BOOK.

NOTES

FOR OTHER FIFTY-MINUTE SELF-STUDY BOOKS
SEE THE BACK OF THIS BOOK.

We hope you enjoyed this book. If so, we have good news for you. This title is part of the best-selling *FIFTY-MINUTE™ Series* of books. All *Series* books are similar in size and identical in price. Several are supported with training videos (identified by the symbol Ⓥ next to the title).

FIFTY-MINUTE Books and Videos are available from your distributor. A free catalog is available upon request from Crisp Publications, Inc., 1200 Hamilton Court, Menlo Park, California 94025.

FIFTY-MINUTE Series Books & Videos organized by general subject area.

Management Training:

Human Resources & Wellness (continued):

Communications & Creativity:

Customer Service/Sales Training:

Small Business & Financial Planning:

Adult Literacy & Learning:

Career/Retirement & Life Planning: